TRAVIS KELCE

★ ALL ACCESS ★

K.C. Kelley

Scholastic Inc

This unauthorized biography was carefully researched to make sure it's accurate. This book is not sponsored by or affiliated with Mr. Kelce or anyone involved with him.

Photos ©: cover: Kara Durrette via AP; insert 1: Steph Chambers/Getty Images; 2 top: Andy Lyons/Getty Images; 2 bottom: Streeter Lecka/Getty Images; 3 top: Alika Jenner/Getty Images; 3 bottom: Jamie Squire/Getty Images; 4 top: Doug Murray/Icon Sportswire via Getty Images; 4 bottom: Cooper Neill/Getty Images; 5 top: Kirby Lee/USA TODAY Sports; 5 center right: AP Photo/Steve Luciano; 5 bottom left: Kohjiro Kinno/Sports Illustrated via Getty Images; 6 top: Kevin Dietsch/Getty Images; 6 bottom left: Peter Aiken/USA TODAY Sports; 6 bottom right: Steph Chambers/Getty Images; 7: Gotham/GC Images/Getty Images; 8: Ezra Shaw/Getty Images. All other photos © Getty Images and Shutterstock.com.

ISBN 978-1-5461-4276-8

10 9 8 7 6 5 4 3 2 1   24 25 26 27 28

Printed in U.S.A.   40
First printing September 2024

Book design by Sarah Salomon for The Story Division
Cover and photo insert design by Lynne Yeamans and Nancy Leonard for The Story Division

TABLE OF CONTENTS

CHAPTER 1: *It's Travis Time!*   1

CHAPTER 2: *A Wild Child*   6

CHAPTER 3: *A Big Bump*   15

CHAPTER 4: *Too Much Fun*   28

CHAPTER 5: *Travis's Turn at the Top*   38

CHAPTER 6: *Two Near Misses*   48

CHAPTER 7: *The Kelce Bowl*   60

CHAPTER 8: *Travis Has a Girlfriend*   73

CHAPTER 1

It's Travis Time!

With more than 120 million people watching (the biggest TV audience in US history!), Travis Kelce reached up and plucked the football from the air. He turned toward the end zone. His team, the Kansas City Chiefs, needed to score a touchdown to win the Super Bowl. A San Francisco 49ers defender banged into Travis . . . and bounced off him.

Two more Niners charged in and smacked Travis. He kept going.

Another 49er snatched at Travis's legs. He kept going.

It took *four* San Francisco players to tackle Travis as he continued to clutch the ball. His fierce determination had put his team three yards from a championship. On the next play, the Chiefs scored, and Travis celebrated. He was a Super Bowl champion (again!) . . . and one of the biggest stories in the world of sports.

Travis Kelce is big in more ways than one. At six feet, five inches and 250 pounds, he's physically big! But he's also big as one of the best tight ends in NFL history. Travis is in the top five of all the biggest stat categories for his position. He's a big personality, too. His winning smile and let's-have-fun attitude have led him to star in TV shows, commercials, and more! And in 2023, he became an even bigger story when he started dating mega-über-superstar Taylor Swift!

That Super Bowl victory over the 49ers in Las Vegas was the third that Travis had earned with the Chiefs. Since he had joined the team in 2013, he had gotten better and better. When quarterback Patrick Mahomes joined the team in 2018, Travis's career really took off.

It was not always an easy road. But like that final play in the Super Bowl, Travis didn't let anything get in his way. He has powered through the same way he powered through tacklers.

With the support of a great family (and his new girlfriend!), Travis has reached the top of the sports world. He has also become an example to anyone who must battle through trouble to reach their goals. And of course, along the way, he has also shown his fans how to have fun!

From backyard games with his brother to

the top of the NFL, from smiling with friends to making millions laugh on *Saturday Night Live*, Travis Kelce has had a pretty amazing life. Let's come along for the ride!

BIG NUMBERS

(Through 2023 NFL Season)

- 3 Super Bowl championships

- 9 Pro Bowl selections

- 11 NFL seasons

- 74 touchdown catches

- 159 NFL games

- 907 receptions

- 11,328 receiving yards

CHAPTER 2

A Wild Child

Jason Kelce didn't know what to do with the little dude born two years after him. Travis the toddler was a mighty handful, and all he wanted to do was play with (and pester) big brother Jason. It was a pattern the pair would continue for years to come.

Travis Michael Kelce was born on October 5, 1989, in Westlake, Ohio, a suburb of Cleveland, and grew up in nearby Cleveland Heights. Jason had been born in 1987 (remember that number!). Both boys were extremely playful and wanted to go, go, go nonstop. Their mom, Donna, said, "Jason and Travis were very active. We had to keep them extremely busy."

On outings at busy amusement parks, Travis was so eager to explore that his mom had to clip a leash to his backpack to keep him safe and close. Both Kelce boys were sent home from preschool for, well . . . for being a little *too* active. Jason poked another kid with a spork, while Travis refused to share the toys!

Home videos from the family show the boys in football gear smacking into each other over and over. Their parents filmed them playing almost every sport imaginable: basketball, hockey, football, and baseball, plus some general Kelce brothers wrestling. They played street hockey against each other, and the driveway was the pitching mound for baseball.

"We were competitive in everything we did," Travis said. "Wiffle ball, card games, even eating dinner." They once tried to see who could throw a football over their house. They both tried, but the result was Football Breaks Window 1, Kelce Brothers 0! "We beat that house up, man," Travis remembered with a laugh.

Sometimes the competition went too far and turned into fights. But after one of those tussles, they stopped. "Jason was a wildebeest growing up, so he was the enforcer," says Travis. "Our last actual fistfight came after a game of basketball. I threw him to the kitchen floor and almost knocked over the stove and almost [ran into] Dad. That was the last one!"

Travis says that he got his competitive nature from his dad, but his great athletic ability from his mom! "Playing ball with my dad . . . fuels the love that I still have for the game," says Travis.

Like Brother, Like Brother

While the boys were similar in their love of sports and scuffling, they were also different. For example, when they got Legos, Travis dove in and started making stuff, while Jason would follow the instructions. Travis loved talking and laughing and having fun. Jason was quieter and didn't like being the center of attention.

By the time Travis was about twelve, he noticed something different about his parents. While he saw that other kids' parents shared a bedroom, his did not. It was an unusual arrangement, but the Kelces did it to make sure their boys got the support they needed.

"If we had split like we had preferred," said Ed Kelce, "trying to get the kids all over the place for sports would have been impossible. Our focus was to help them find their passion and then help them feed whatever that passion was."

The Kelces did not divorce until both boys were out of college.

As for the Kelce brothers' passion, it was all sports, all the time. Travis played hockey in junior high, and then basketball and football in high school. In fact, he says he started playing football to follow Jason.

"I saw him playing sports and so I wanted to do it, too. I still always feel like a little brother around him, and I think I can always learn from him," said Travis years later.

Travis was a quarterback on the freshman team at Cleveland Heights High School. After that, he was excited about his sophomore season, because he would get to play on the same team as Jason, who would be a senior. But Travis failed French class. Without good grades, he could not play on the team. He was crushed.

"I always wanted to feel that power tandem of me and my brother out there fighting against the world. It was an embarrassing time, knowing I should have been helping my brother shine in his senior year," said Travis.

But as a junior, he buckled down, passed French class (and all his others), and became the team's quarterback. He also watched Jason head off to play at the University of Cincinnati.

Travis's coach, Jeff Rotsky, was amazed at his QB's all-around skill. "One word: Wow! I'd never seen a player [his size] who could run, jump, and have ball skills like that." Another coach called him "the best athlete in town."

Rotsky also admired Travis for coming back from his disappointment as a sophomore. "[He] didn't put his head in his pillow.

He didn't cry about it, and he made some mistakes and came back stronger and was better for it."

Super Senior Season

As a senior, Travis threw for more than 1,500 yards and 15 touchdowns. He also rushed for more than 1,000 yards and scored 10 times, showing the speed and tackle-breaking skills that would make him a star. Travis was also a top player on the basketball team.

Today, Cleveland Heights students walk past the framed, signed jerseys of Travis and Jason, wondering if they, too, can make their NFL dreams come true. As his senior season ended, Travis announced that he would (gee, surprise!) follow Jason to the University of Cincinnati. Would the brothers finally get a chance to play together?

FAVORITE FOODS

According to Kumar Ferguson, these are Travis's favorite things to eat. Kumar has been friends with Travis since they were kids and has been his personal chef for many years.

- Oatmeal with fresh fruit

- French toast (pregame meal!)

- Seafood alfredo

- Hot wings

- Steak fillet

- Pineapple pizza

- BONUS: Travis's *least* favorite food is MAYONNAISE! Donna Kelce also says that Travis and Jason could each eat a whole chicken in one sitting!

FUN FACT

Travis is multi-talented: His high school coach once said Travis could have been a college star at baseball, basketball, or hockey! And when Travis had to miss a year of college football, he played baseball to stay in shape.

CHAPTER 3

A Big Bump

Not long after Travis graduated from high school, Coach Rotsky gave him some advice that sounded later like he was using a crystal ball. He knew that Travis wanted to play quarterback in college, but the coach predicted his former player might find a different path.

"Listen, they see you as a quarterback," Rotsky told Travis. "But . . . if you're not the [starting quarterback] there, you're going to be an unbelievable tight end. And that's probably what's going to happen."

Let's see if the coach was right!

In the fall of 2008, Travis moved to Cincinnati, ready to take on the world. He was looking forward to being together with Jason again, both on and off the field. But when he got to the team, he was told that he would be taking the year off. The Cincinnati Bearcats had too many quarterbacks. He was just a freshman, the youngest, so he would take what's called a "redshirt" year. That meant that he could practice with the team and attend home games, but he could not play. Travis worked hard so that the coaches would remember him next year, when he could play.

First Cincy TD

When the 2009 season rolled around, Travis was ready. He was still not a starting player, however. Other quarterbacks were set to play before him. But, he was still a good runner, and in the team's first game of 2009, Travis got a big chance.

In football, when a player other than the QB lines up behind the center, it's known as a Wildcat formation. Against Rutgers, the Bearcats sent Travis in to be the Wildcat. They were on the 16-yard line. Travis got the ball and charged ahead, following his blockers. One of them was Jason, who was playing left guard. Travis put his hand on Jason's back and followed him—like always! They ended up in the end zone for Travis's first college touchdown. Later in the game, he scored again on a short run.

"That was one of the coolest moments of my life, sharing a field with my brother," Travis said later.

But the Bearcats did not use him again until the final game of the season, the Sugar

Bowl against Florida State. He ran the ball once and gained 19 yards. After the game, he and his teammates enjoyed being in New Orleans. As it turned out, he enjoyed it too much. Not long after returning to Cincinnati, he was called into the office of Coach Bruce Jones.

A Major Roadblock

"He said, 'Son, you're off the team. I'm taking your scholarship.'" Travis was in tears. "I felt empty." It turned out that Travis had broken team rules in New Orleans.

"I had to figure it out or I was going to be stuck back in Cleveland, trying to tell the story of what could have been," said Travis.

He would have to keep a 3.0 grade point average and not miss a single class. He would also have to find a way to pay for school. Travis found a part-time job as a telemarketer and got help from his parents to pay for books. More importantly, Jason made him move into a house he was sharing.

"I think it was the best thing that ever happened to him," Jason said later. "He had never had to overcome something to have to work hard."

"I let a lot of people down, especially my brother," remembered Travis years later. "But he was every bit a mentor for me. I knew Jason had gone to the coaches and told them that if I got a second chance I wouldn't let them down." It was just like high school and his French class. When Travis stumbled, Jason was there to pick him up.

Travis soon found another problem to overcome. Coach Rotsky's prediction was true—the coaches wanted him to switch positions and become a tight end. Travis knew that this was his last chance; so he put aside his dream of being a quarterback and dove into his new role.

He had to learn how to catch passes, block opponents, and run passing routes. He had to learn how to plant his feet to make moves and how to avoid pass defenders. The coaches worked with him every day, sometimes staying after practice was over to help him improve.

Travis worked hard off the field, too. As a junior, he made the dean's list (an academic honor roll) for the first time.

"He had to work every day. Every day there were struggles and triumphs, but in two years he became a changed individual on and off the field," said Coach Jones, the same person who had kicked Travis off the team a year earlier.

"I knew heading into his senior year that he

could accomplish great things," Jones continued. "You saw the true Travis Kelce come out in terms of leadership, toughness, and effort. He set the standard of what we believed in our football program."

Super Senior Season—Again

Travis became the centerpiece of the offense. Bearcats passers looked for their big tight end whenever they were in trouble. Travis caught a pass in every one of the team's games, while snagging a team-high 8 touchdown catches. When the regular season was over, he had piled up 722 receiving yards, setting a school record for tight end. His 45 catches were the most by any player on the Bearcats. They were also the most by any tight end in the sport's top division.

Travis's last college game was his best. In

the Belk Bowl, a postseason matchup with Duke, Travis had five catches for 123 yards. The highlight was an 83-yard touchdown run on which he outraced the Duke defenders to the end zone.

In 2011, Jason had been chosen in the NFL Draft by the Philadelphia Eagles. Once again, Travis wanted to follow his brother. He gathered with his family and friends to watch the Draft on TV and waited for his name to be called as the newest member of an NFL team. It took longer than he thought. Four other tight ends were called. Travis began to worry.

"Why [didn't] a team just take a chance on me?" he said later.

Donna watched her son get sadder and sadder. "It was very humbling. He thought he was better than all the tight ends picked ahead of him."

Then the phone rang. It was Coach Andy Reid of the Kansas City Chiefs. He asked Travis, "Are you going to mess up this opportunity if I take you?" Travis said, no, he wouldn't. And then Coach Reid asked to speak with Jason, who had played for Reid in Philadelphia.

"He asked me which Kelce he'd be getting, the one who got kicked off a team or the one who excelled as a senior," said Jason. "I told Coach that I was vouching for him and he was getting the best tight end in the draft."

Travis got back on the phone and Reid told him, "Welcome to the Kansas City Chiefs."

Travis had made it. He had overcome different obstacles and was ready to become a professional.

But then there was a new hurdle. Travis hurt his knee in the summer of 2013 and had to miss almost his whole rookie season. During those long months of recovery, Travis faced doubts and setbacks. Was this the end of his NFL dream? Or would he overcome like he always had?

FUN FACT

Travis's father's family pronounces their last name "KELSE"—rhymes with "or else!" But so many people said it wrong, they just stick with "KELL-see."

So What Is a Tight End, Anyway?

Travis's position, tight end (TE), is part of the Chiefs offense. In football, the players at the far sides of the offensive line used to be called "ends." Today, they are called wide receivers. But the receiver who starts closest to the other linemen is called the tight end—tight meaning closest, not closest fitting!

Here's a quick look at what tight ends do:

1. BLOCK

On running plays, the TE runs in front of the ball carrier. The TE tries to knock down or push aside the other team's defenders to give the runner space to go! If another player catches a pass, the TE might be able to block for that teammate, too.

2. GO OUT FOR PASSES

On passing plays, the quarterback tells the TE what route he should run. The TE follows that route, trying to stay away from defenders.

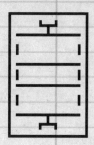

3. CATCH PASSES If the QB

chooses to pass the ball toward the TE . . . he better catch it!

4. RUN! If the TE catches a pass,

he runs as far down the field as he can before he is tackled or knocked out of bounds.

5. RUN, PART 2 On a few

plays, the QB hands the ball to the TE, who then runs as far as he can.

6. CELEBRATE! When a TE

(or any player) scores a touchdown, it's time to dance and celebrate!

CHAPTER 4

Too Much Fun

Early in his first NFL season, before he even played a single game, Travis had to have surgery on his knee. The operation meant that he would miss the whole 2013 season. He was frustrated but knew that it was something he could come back from. Travis worked hard to get in shape, and once he took the field in 2014, he took off!

In the Chiefs' third game of that season, Travis was the starting tight end and he caught his first NFL TD pass. He would add four

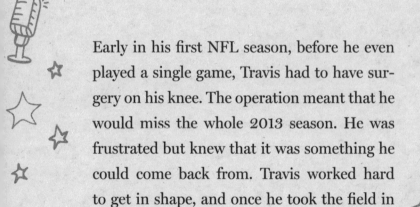

The San Francisco 49ers defense converges on Travis as he sets up the winning touchdown in overtime in the SUPER BOWL IN 2024!

Travis's last game with Cincinnati was his best yet, and he got his hands on the BELK BOWL TROPHY.

GO!

Travis's star continued to rise as Kansas City Chiefs tight end during a FANTASTIC 2019 SEASON.

Bathing in Arrowhead Stadium's famous SEA OF RED, Travis basks in the love of his hometown crowd.

SPLASH! Continuing a famous football tradition, Travis and his teammates douse coach Andy Reid with Gatorade after the Chiefs' Super Bowl win in 2020.

Travis and BIG BROTHER JASON reflect after playing against each other in the Super Bowl.

"MAMA KELCE" shows her support for Travis and Jason on the field at the Super Bowl.

Look at the colors and logos and even uniform numbers here.

Travis's mom, DONNA, wore an outfit that represented both her sons as they played against each other in the Super Bowl.

Why 46?
Because Biden
is the 46th
president!

Travis and quarterback Patrick Mahomes
pose with President Biden while visiting
THE WHITE HOUSE after the Chiefs'
Super Bowl win over the Eagles.

On June 15, 2023, Travis received
his first Super Bowl ring at a ceremony
in Kansas City.

Travis is known for having fun with
his game-day outfits, including this
custom SPARKLY BLACK SUIT that
he wore to the Super Bowl in 2024.

A smiling Travis enjoys date night with singing superstar TAYLOR SWIFT.

Travis celebrates his Super Bowl LVIII win on the field with girlfriend TAYLOR SWIFT.

more in 2014. His 67 catches for 862 yards were both tops on the team.

Travis was still growing up, though. The Chiefs had given him a bonus worth more than $700,000, plus they would pay him $3 million over his first three seasons. Being Travis, he had fun with the money, buying classic cars and $10,000 sneakers. He traveled a lot while he was not playing, enjoying restaurants, shows, and more. He kept improving on the field, though. In 2015, he caught 72 passes and scored five times; he also was named to his first Pro Bowl, which is the NFL's annual all-star squad.

Travis the TV Star

In the summer of 2016, Travis found another way to make money: He became a TV star. The young tight end starred in *Catching*

Kelce, a reality show. Women from every state competed to go on dates with Travis, and he was supposed to choose one at the end of the show. It was not a big hit at the time.

"It was kind of like *The Bachelor*, except instead of roses, I handed out footballs, and instead of watching, people did not," Travis joked later. Looking back, Travis thinks the experience helped him learn to deal with media attention, which he would need in the years ahead. (His teammates still teased him about it, though. Quarterback Patrick Mahomes once said the Chiefs named a play after the show!)

Like his love for football, Travis's love for the spotlight started back in Cleveland Heights. "My mom's home videos, man, just having the camera on me at all times," Travis remembers. "Honestly, I've always been comfortable in the rooms I've been in. I've been able to look into a camera with ease, just having fun."

Travis began to mature. With some of the money he was making, he founded the 87 and Running Foundation to support kids in need. Travis donated to it each time he made a catch. He also made appearances and held events to raise more money. "I wanted to give back, both where I come from and [to] the city I'm in now," Travis said. "I wanted to make a difference in the best way possible and the only way I could think of was my impact on the youth."

In 2016, Travis had his best season yet. He had 85 catches and topped 1,000 yards receiving for the first time, with a total of 1,125. He was a Pro Bowler again and was named to the First Team All-NFL squad, a big honor.

Travis was becoming well known in football, not only for his pass-catching skills, but also for his end zone dances. Every time he scored, he would come up with a new dance, showing off pretty good moves before joining teammates in celebration.

"In the end zone, I turn into a happy-go-lucky kid. I'm just going to go ahead and dance this off! I got moves for days!" he once bragged.

FUN FACT

"Sports, for me, was where I built my confidence. I was a shy kid growing up until I got on the sports field or the court or the ice rink. Then, I let my personality show more because I was having fun, having success. That kind of propelled me to have confidence in life."

Brother vs. Brother, Part 1

Travis's Chiefs and Jason's Eagles had played each other in 2013, but Travis was injured and did not get into the game. That meant that a 2017 matchup for the teams would be the first time the two Kelce brothers faced each other on the football field . . . and not in the backyard! (Spoiler alert: It would not be the last time!) Their parents were in the stands, but who would they root for? Donna wore a shirt that was half-Eagles and half-Chiefs. Ed wore a Cincinnati Bearcats jersey with Travis's college number 18 on the front and Jason's number 60 on the back.

The score was tied in the fourth quarter when Chiefs' QB Alex Smith threw a pass to Travis from the 15-yard line. Travis motored toward the goal line. When he got to about the five-yard line, he leaped for the end zone. An Eagles defender got underneath him, and together the pair flew almost ten yards through the air! Travis landed with the go-ahead touchdown. To celebrate (and to tease Jason), he ran down the field flapping his arms like an eagle!

"Part of me was furious, because the other team had scored, but part of me was like, wow, that was amazing," Jason said. The Chiefs went on to win the game 27–20. Travis led the team with 8 catches for 103 yards. Afterward, the two brothers met on the field and exchanged jerseys. After planting a smooch on his big brother's face, Travis told Jason for the first time why he had chosen jersey number 87: Because that's the year Jason was born.

One Brother Makes It to the Top

The 2017 regular season ended with Travis having another great year. His 8 touchdowns were the most he had scored at that point (of course, he had eight new dances to show off, too!). The Chiefs lost in the playoffs, but Jason and the Eagles made it to the Super Bowl. Jason's powerful blocking helped pave the way for Philadelphia's first NFL championship since 1960. Travis was at the game in Minnesota, cheering on his big brother.

"To see him reach that mountaintop was awesome," Travis said. At the Eagles' victory parade, Jason channeled a bit of his little brother's enthusiasm. He wore a wild purple-gold-green turban costume and gave a rousing and hilarious speech to the huge crowd.

"I hope that he remains as happy as he is now, and that he only wins one Super Bowl and I win the rest!" Travis said afterward.

Would Travis get his wish?

CHAPTER 5

Travis's Turn at the Top

In 2018, everything changed for Travis—
but this time, the change was positive. The
Chiefs welcomed a new quarterback, Patrick
Mahomes. The young passer had played one
game in 2017, but in 2018, he became the
starter. He was a tremendous athlete, able to
pass extraordinarily well and escape tacklers as
a runner. His father had been a Major League
Baseball pitcher and had taught Patrick how
to throw. Patrick soon was amazing fans and
opponents with backhanded throws, left-
handed passes, and no-look targets.

For Travis, it was the beginning of a beautiful friendship. The two players quickly found that their styles worked together perfectly. They admired each other's ability to work hard and prepare for games. Once the action started, both players were athletic and creative. When Patrick was being chased by pass rushers, he knew Travis would find a way to get open for him.

"Travis is definitely the best player I've thrown to," Patrick said. "With how big he is and the way he is able to run routes and make plays happen, [he] is a really rare thing."

In 2018, their first full season together, Travis had his best season yet. He had career highs with 103 catches, 1,336 receiving yards, and 10 touchdown catches. Of course, he made another Pro Bowl.

By the end of that same season, Patrick was the NFL leader with 50 touchdown passes, only the third player ever to reach that total.

He threw for an incredible 5,097 yards and was named the NFL Offensive Player of the Year and Most Valuable Player.

Together, Travis and Patrick led the Chiefs to the playoffs, one game away from the Super Bowl, losing the American Football Conference (AFC) Championship Game in overtime to the New England Patriots. That team, of course, was led by its own legendary quarterback, Tom Brady.

With all the attention the Chiefs were getting in the playoffs, fans started noticing another part of Travis's personality. It turned out that he loved dressing up! Before each game, players arrive at the stadium, tracked by dozens of cameras. Many guys take the opportunity to bring out their favorite outfits, stylish shoes, and designer sunglasses. Travis took part with his own personal style.

"I've always been into fashion, into ways to express yourself and show your creativity," says Travis. "I wear it all to put a smile on someone's face." Along with those expensive kicks he got as a rookie, Travis says he now owns almost 400 pairs of shoes!

To the Top!

The Chiefs' success in 2018 set the stage for a fantastic 2019 season. They won their first four games, scoring at least 28 points in each. Then they lost three of their next six games. A promising season was fading quickly. Then Kansas City beat the LA Chargers, helped by a touchdown catch from Travis. That started a six-game winning streak that gave the Chiefs a 12–4 record, second-best in the AFC.

In the first round of the playoffs, KC faced the Houston Texans and soon found themselves in big trouble. They trailed 24–0 early in the second quarter. It's very hard to come back from that many points in the NFL, especially in the playoffs. But not every team has Travis and Patrick. After the Chiefs scored to make it 24–7, the super-duo went to work.

Mahomes to Kelce, 5 yards—touchdown!

Two minutes later, Mahomes to Kelce, 6 yards—touchdown!

With less than a minute left in the first half, Mahomes to Kelce, 5 yards—touchdown!

Travis's third touchdown of the quarter gave the Chiefs the lead. They never looked back, piling on the points for what became a 51–31 win and one of the biggest comebacks in NFL history. As we've seen, don't ever count Travis Kelce out, no matter what happens!

In the AFC Championship Game, the Tennessee Titans double-covered Travis. They were not going to let him beat them. That was fine with Travis. He watched his teammates, wide receivers Tyreek Hill and Sammy

Watkins, get more room to run. They scored three times between them. Kansas City was off to the Super Bowl!

Finally the Champ

In Super Bowl LIV, the Chiefs faced the San Francisco 49ers. Once again, they fell behind and had to come back. As usual, Travis was a big part of the team's success.

The Chiefs trailed the 49ers by 10 points with about six minutes left in the fourth quarter when Patrick aimed a pass toward Travis in the end zone. The only thing a 49ers defender could do was knock Travis down—pass interference! That gave the Chiefs the ball at the 1-yard line. Guess who caught the TD pass on the next play! That brought the Chiefs to within three points.

Mahomes then led the team to two late touchdowns. When the final whistle blew, the

Chiefs were the NFL champions for the first time since 1969. Chiefs 31, 49ers 20.

Travis celebrated with his family and friends after the game. He had a big hug for Ed and another for Donna. He danced with Mahomes and other Chiefs teammates. Of course, now that he was a big celebrity, he had some famous fans, too. He hugged actor Paul Rudd (you know . . . Ant-Man?) on the field after the game.

During a postgame interview, Travis was already looking to top his big brother. He boasted that his speech at the parade would be louder and wilder than Jason's famous speech. A moment later, live on TV, Jason grabbed him from behind in a big hug.

"I've never been so nervous in my life [as] in that fourth quarter," said Jason.

Nervous? Why? The Chiefs had Travis Kelce!

Later, Travis thought about his brother's Super Bowl win and the road they both had traveled.

"It was a very weird feeling for me when I won the Super Bowl," said Travis. "There had been a moment I had not made [Jason] proud, but then there was a moment that I did. I owe a lot to that big bear. Without him, I don't know what I would be doing."

But Travis was not done doing what he was doing!

TRAVIS . . . LIVE!

During Super Bowl LVI, Travis and Patrick wore microphones on the field. Here are some of their most memorable quotes:

- Travis to Patrick before the game: "I'm here for you all day, baby!"

- To 49ers tight end George Kittle: "Let's make this one forever, baby!"

- Patrick: "I'm a beast! I'm a beast!"

- Travis to his teammates: "Let's go! Let's go! Let's go! Let's go! Let's go! Let's go!"

- Patrick (still trailing late in the game): "They're going to be talking about this one forever."

- Travis (after dumping Gatorade on Coach Reid): "Let's go! Fire up, baby! Congrats, big guy! Been a long time comin'!"

- Ed (over Travis's mic): "I'm so proud of you. You've worked so hard your whole life."

- Travis (holding Lombardi Trophy): "This is so beautiful, man!"

FASHION TRENDSETTER TRAV

Here are some details of some of Travis's more famous outfits:

- An all-red suit (wore to the White House in 2023)

- Leopard-print high-top sneakers and snake-skin cowboy boots

- Blue brocade suit (fancy swirly stitching!)

- A light purple suit with big white checks

- Kid Super furry long coat and a yellow zebra-stripe coat

- Fun shirts and sweaters that feature koi, pineapples, tigers, and more

- Outfits from Louis Vuitton, Gucci, Dior, and more!

- Piano pants!

CHAPTER 6

Two Near Misses

How much do the Chiefs love Travis? Before the 2020 season, they signed him to a new contract. They agreed to pay him $57 million to play through the 2025 season. (After that, who knows?) How much do opponents love Travis? Not at all!

As great as he had been already, Travis reached new heights in 2020. He scored in each of the team's first two games, then had 2 touchdowns in a big win over the Buffalo Bills. Even as every defense lined up to stop

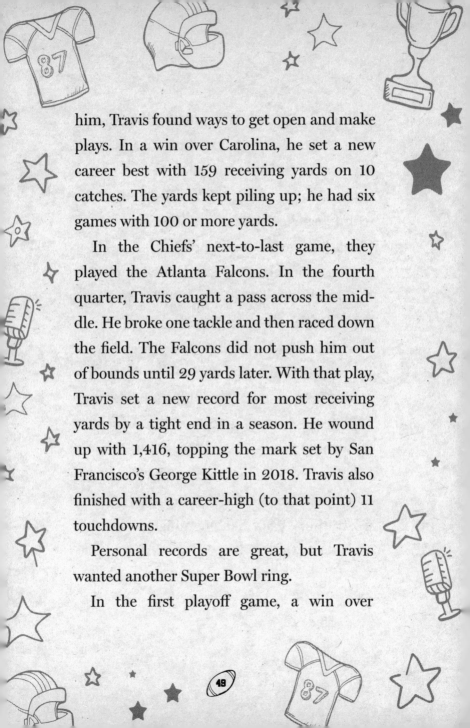

him, Travis found ways to get open and make plays. In a win over Carolina, he set a new career best with 159 receiving yards on 10 catches. The yards kept piling up; he had six games with 100 or more yards.

In the Chiefs' next-to-last game, they played the Atlanta Falcons. In the fourth quarter, Travis caught a pass across the middle. He broke one tackle and then raced down the field. The Falcons did not push him out of bounds until 29 yards later. With that play, Travis set a new record for most receiving yards by a tight end in a season. He wound up with 1,416, topping the mark set by San Francisco's George Kittle in 2018. Travis also finished with a career-high (to that point) 11 touchdowns.

Personal records are great, but Travis wanted another Super Bowl ring.

In the first playoff game, a win over

Cleveland, Travis had 8 catches, including a touchdown. Next up, the Bills. Travis must like playing them, because he caught 2 touchdown passes . . . again! He also led both teams with 13 catches in the game. The win sent the Chiefs back to the Super Bowl!

Unfortunately, they faced the Tampa Bay Buccaneers, led by Tom Brady. The Bucs kept the Chiefs from scoring many points. Travis more than did his part. He had 10 catches for 133 yards. That was the most ever by a tight end in a Super Bowl. His third straight 100-yard postseason game was also a record for tight ends.

The records didn't matter. Travis was disappointed he and the Chiefs lost, 31–9. "It was frustrating. It felt like anything we did they had an answer for," he said afterward.

Keeping Busy

In the offseason, Travis continued doing more work in front of cameras. No new reality shows, but he appeared in more commercials. Companies loved his famous face and his outgoing personality. He has made ads for soup, insurance, sandwiches, and hardware stores. One ad for McDonald's even featured Travis's touchdown dances! He was in ads for streaming TV services and for different NFL programs like *NFL Play*, which encouraged kids to try the sport (or just be active!). Over the next few years, he added more companies to his crowded calendar. In 2023, Travis rolled up his sleeve and filmed an ad encouraging people to get their COVID-19 vaccines. By the fall of 2023, he and teammate Patrick Mahomes were the two most popular NFL "pitchmen," appearing in more than 375 commercials during that season.

Travis also played a lot of golf, his new offseason hobby. In 2023, he teamed up with Patrick in a big made-for-TV game. They faced off against Stephen Curry and Klay Thompson of the Golden State Warriors basketball team. The Chiefs won that one, too!

When he's not filming ads or playing golf, Travis spends some time in the offseason checking out expensive, fancy cars. He already owns an Aston Martin Vanquish, a Cadillac Escalade, a fancy SUV called a Range Rover, and a Rolls-Royce Ghost. He also owns a souped-up Chevy Chevelle from 1970. One report said his cars are worth well over a million dollars!

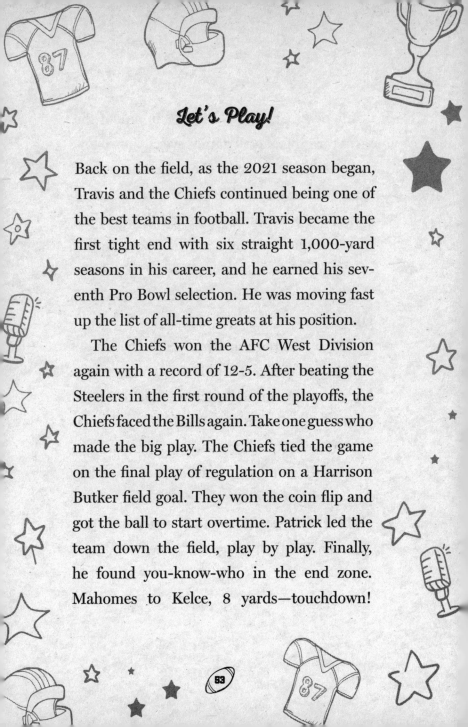

Let's Play!

Back on the field, as the 2021 season began, Travis and the Chiefs continued being one of the best teams in football. Travis became the first tight end with six straight 1,000-yard seasons in his career, and he earned his seventh Pro Bowl selection. He was moving fast up the list of all-time greats at his position.

The Chiefs won the AFC West Division again with a record of 12-5. After beating the Steelers in the first round of the playoffs, the Chiefs faced the Bills again. Take one guess who made the big play. The Chiefs tied the game on the final play of regulation on a Harrison Butker field goal. They won the coin flip and got the ball to start overtime. Patrick led the team down the field, play by play. Finally, he found you-know-who in the end zone. Mahomes to Kelce, 8 yards—touchdown!

Game over! Chiefs 42, Bills 36 in one of the most thrilling playoff games ever.

Kansas City faced the Cincinnati Bengals in the AFC Championship Game. Travis scored again, and the Chiefs again tied the game on the final play. But in overtime, they ran out of magic. The Bengals intercepted a pass by Patrick, then drove to a game-winning field goal.

Travis was bummed but knew the Chiefs could win again. "I think right now, everybody is more motivated now than we were before we won a Super Bowl," he said later. "I think everybody has still got a bad taste in our mouth on how we finished the season last year, and it's just that's fueling the fire."

That fire would soon burn through the National Football League!

FUN FACT

Remember how Travis played QB in college? In the NFL, he has tried three passes on trick plays. He completed one . . . but also threw an interception on one in 2017! Oops! In 2021, he threw a touchdown pass in a playoff win over the Steelers!

TRAVIS'S TOP TEN GAMES

In order by date

⬭ **October 21, 2018   vs. Bengals**
Career-best average of 19 yards per catch

⬭ **December 2, 2018   vs. Raiders**
Career-best tie 12 catches for 168 yards and 2 TDs

⬭ **January 12, 2020   vs. Texans**
3 TDs and 134 yards in big playoff comeback win

⬭ **November 11, 2020   vs. Chargers**
3 of his 6 catches went for TDs

⬭ **January 24, 2021   vs. Bills**
13 catches for 118 yards and 2 TDs in big playoff win

February 7, 2021   **vs. Buccaneers**
133 yards, new Super Bowl record for TEs

December 16, 2021   **vs. Chargers**
Career-best 191 receiving yards on 13 catches

October 10, 2022   **vs. Raiders**
Only 25 receiving yards but 4 TDs!

January 21, 2023   **vs. Jaguars**
Postseason-best 14 catches, plus 2 TDs

January 28, 2024   **vs. Ravens**
Becomes all-time postseason catch leader

TALKIN' 'BOUT TRAVIS

What do the other Chiefs have to say about Travis Kelce? Read on to find out!

"[His rise in fame has] been cool to watch for me. Obviously, he has all that attention, but he's just been himself the whole time. He still will walk through the stadium and treat every single person like they're his best friend."
—Chiefs QB Patrick Mahomes

"He's somebody I respect greatly. He's somebody that gets the offense and the defense excited and ready to play each week. He brings a level of charisma that very few people have."
—Clark Hunt, Chiefs owner

"Let me just tell you: Travis Kelce is my favorite teammate of all-time. On any level: Pop Warner, high school, college . . . He took his time trying to teach me the role of being the tight end. Being in a room with Kelce these last few years has been an extraordinary blessing to my game."
—Former Chiefs (now Dolphins) TE Jody Fortson

"He brings energy every day. I've been lucky enough to coach him and his brother and they're both that way. They're just wired where they want to be the best, but yet enjoy playing the game like no other."
—Chiefs coach Andy Reid

"We have the best player to ever play this game at that position. He's still the best tight end in the game."
—Chiefs WR Marquez Valdes-Scantling

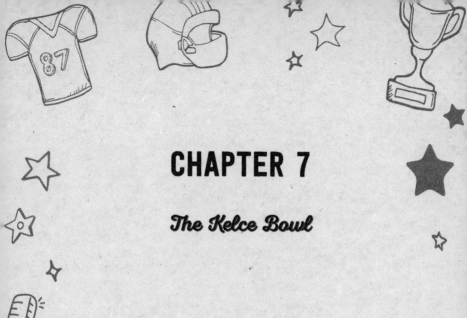

CHAPTER 7

The Kelce Bowl

The summer before the 2022 NFL season was a busy one for Travis. By taking classes online, he earned enough credits to finally earn his degree from the University of Cincinnati. (In a documentary, Jason teased Travis for missing a flight . . . and missing the graduation ceremony!) Travis's foundation also began a new program at the school to support athletes' mental health, a move based on his own experience.

"The transition from high school to college was a difficult one; it was an emotional roller

coaster at times," said Travis. "Being able to have that support system in place is part of the reason why I decided to start this [program] and give back to my alma mater and its athletic department."

Then in September, as the season began, Travis and Jason started *New Heights*, a weekly podcast. It was basically the two brothers just chatting about football, life, and each other. It became very popular very quickly. Travis continued his upbeat, lots-of-laughs style, helping Jason come out of his gruff and grumbly shell. Listeners ate up their tales of growing up. They also loved hearing inside-the-huddle stories from two of the NFL's best players.

The brothers shared stories about their childhood, what hamburgers they liked, their favorite types of music, and even how their parents met. The Kelces welcomed guests, too, including their own quarterbacks: Mahomes for the Chiefs and Jalen

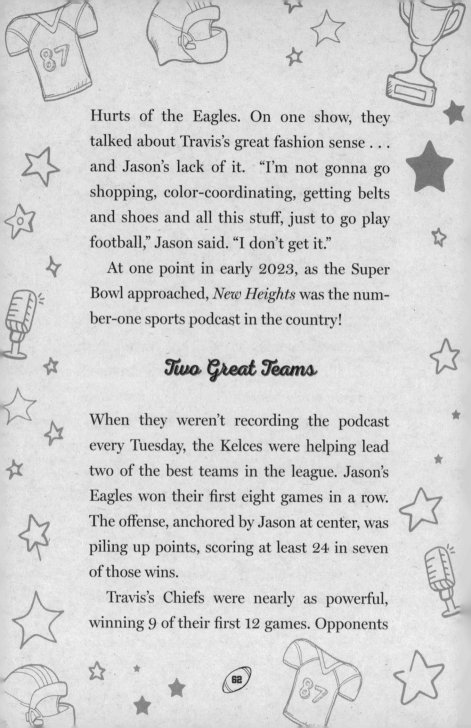

Hurts of the Eagles. On one show, they talked about Travis's great fashion sense . . . and Jason's lack of it. "I'm not gonna go shopping, color-coordinating, getting belts and shoes and all this stuff, just to go play football," Jason said. "I don't get it."

At one point in early 2023, as the Super Bowl approached, *New Heights* was the number-one sports podcast in the country!

Two Great Teams

When they weren't recording the podcast every Tuesday, the Kelces were helping lead two of the best teams in the league. Jason's Eagles won their first eight games in a row. The offense, anchored by Jason at center, was piling up points, scoring at least 24 in seven of those wins.

Travis's Chiefs were nearly as powerful, winning 9 of their first 12 games. Opponents were having trouble stopping the Chiefs offense. Travis was having some of the best games of his career. He had 121 receiving yards and a touchdown in the team's 44–21 win over the Arizona Cardinals to open the season. In a 30–29 win over the Las Vegas Raiders, Travis caught 4 touchdown passes! That was his most ever in an NFL game, and second most by a tight end in NFL history. In a later game, Travis had 3 more TD catches.

The Chiefs finished 14-3. That was the most wins in a season in team history. It also was tied for the best record in the NFL in 2022 . . . with the Eagles!

In the playoffs, the Eagles relied on their defense. They gave up only 7 points in each of two wins, 38–7 over the New York Giants and 31–7 over the San Francisco 49ers. Quarterback Jalen Hurts had a touchdown run in each game, following Jason's blocking. (His TD against the 49ers came on the

"Brotherly Shove," a short-yardage play. Hurts got the ball and dove forward behind Jason. Two other Eagles then pushed Hurts from behind! The play's name came from a nickname for Philadelphia: the City of Brotherly Love.)

Meanwhile, the Chiefs had a tougher time in the playoffs. They beat the Jaguars and Bengals but gave up 20 points to each. Kansas City needed a game-winning field goal on the final play to win the AFC Championship Game over the Bengals. Of course, Travis scored in that game, too!

When the playoffs were over, the Kelce family was very, very excited . . . and a bit confused. For the first time in NFL history, a pair of brothers would face off in the Super Bowl. Jason's Eagles would play Travis's Chiefs in Super Bowl LVII (that's 57 in regular numbers).

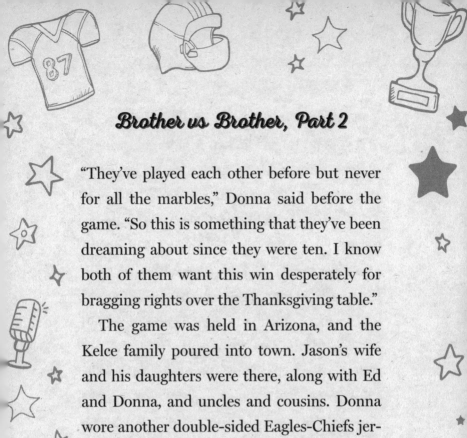

Brother vs Brother, Part 2

"They've played each other before but never for all the marbles," Donna said before the game. "So this is something that they've been dreaming about since they were ten. I know both of them want this win desperately for bragging rights over the Thanksgiving table."

The game was held in Arizona, and the Kelce family poured into town. Jason's wife and his daughters were there, along with Ed and Donna, and uncles and cousins. Donna wore another double-sided Eagles-Chiefs jersey again (after the game, it wound up in the Pro Football Hall of Fame in Canton, Ohio, not far from the Kelces' hometown).

"I'm rooting for the offense," Donna joked, knowing that both of her boys played for the offense of their teams!

The game turned out to be one of the most exciting in Super Bowl history. Travis caught a TD pass in the first quarter to tie the score at 7–7. The Eagles kicked a field goal to end the second half with a 24–14 lead. The offensive fireworks continued in the second half. Kansas City took its first lead of the game, 28–27, after a Patrick Mahomes TD pass. But after another KC TD, Hurts pounded in from the two-yard line to tie the score.

The back-and-forth game probably would be won by the last team with the ball. And that team was the Chiefs. Mahomes led a drive toward the Eagles' end zone. Travis caught one of three passes Mahomes completed. The Chiefs reached the Eagles' nine-yard line. With less than ten seconds left, Butker booted a field goal. After one final Eagles' play, it was over. The Chiefs had won the "Kelce Bowl," 38–35.

Travis celebrated with his teammates, shouting for joy and tossing his helmet. He hugged Coach Reid and Mahomes and all the other receivers. But he was looking for one person in particular. A few moments after the game, the Kelce brothers hugged it out on the field as confetti flew and music blared.

"I love you, man, congratulations," said Jason.

"I love you. What a year!" answered Travis.

After the game, Travis added, "It's the greatest feeling in the world, being here with the guys we did it with, and the coaches we did it with, through all the adversity," he said. "All I know is that we're coming back next year with the right mindset on trying to get another one."

But first, Travis had to get famous.

National Spotlight

On March 4, 2023, Travis hosted *Saturday Night Live*, the famous late-night comedy show. On the air since 1975, *SNL* is one of the most famous TV shows ever. Many athletes had been the guest host, including Peyton Manning, Michael Jordan, LeBron James, Dwayne "The Rock" Johnson, and Derek Jeter. Travis's love of the spotlight and upbeat personality made him a natural to join the list. Being a Super Bowl champ meant that most viewers knew who he was, too!

As the host, he had to open with a short speech, called a monologue. And he was funny! He made jokes about football and his brother and even did an impression of Mahomes! Travis was also in skits. In one, he took his American Girl doll to lunch. In another, he was a self-defense teacher who went a little too far in demonstrating moves. Travis had a terrific time, and the *SNL* producers said he was a natural talent.

On April 26, the NFL Draft was held in Kansas City. Travis and Jason put on a live show of *New Heights* for 10,000 fans in person and millions more listeners. Mahomes, Reid, and NFL Commissioner Roger Goodell (he got booed!) were among the guests.

Travis got more headlines when the Super Bowl–champion Chiefs visited the White House to be honored by President Joe Biden. Travis being Travis, he pretended to jump ahead of the president to take the microphone!

In July, Travis talked about a topic on the podcast that would soon sweep the country, if not the world. He said that he had tried to get his phone number to a certain international megastar singer. Eventually, he did . . . and everything changed again.

FAMOUS NFL BROTHERS

The Kelces are the only brothers to face each other in a Super Bowl. But other brothers have had great NFL careers. Here are some of the best:

⬭ **Eli and Peyton Manning:** Sons of NFL QB Archie Manning, this pair of passers each won two Super Bowls and two Super Bowl MVP. Peyton was also a five-time NFL MVP and holds the single-season passing TD record with 55 in 2013.

⬭ **J.J., T.J., and Derek Watt:** No QB wanted to see these brothers heading their way. J.J. was a three-time Defensive Player of the Year and an all-time sack master. T.J. was the 2021 DPOY and set a single-season record with 22.5 sacks. Oh, yes, and brother Derek had a seven-year NFL career as a running back!

Shannon and Sterling Sharpe: Sterling was a seven-year wide receiver who led the NFL in TD catches twice for the Green Bay Packers. "Little" brother Shannon was a Hall of Famer, one of the best tight ends ever, and a three-time Super Bowl champion.

Tiki and Ronde Barber: They're not just brothers, they're twins! Tiki was a running back for the New York Giants and had six 1,000-yard seasons. Ronde was a defensive back who made five Pro Bowls and was elected to the Pro Football Hall of Fame.

TRAVIS SELLS!

Here are some of the companies and products for which Travis has done ads of one sort or another:

- Campbell's Soup
- Dick's Sporting Goods
- DirecTV
- Experian
- McDonald's
- Nike
- Old Spice
- Pfizer
- State Farm
- Walgreens

CHAPTER 8

Travis Has a Girlfriend!

Travis Kelce liked Taylor Swift. He liked her music and he wanted to meet her. He even went to one of her concerts with a friendship bracelet with his phone number on it, intending to give it to her!

Sometime in August 2023, mutual friends connected the two and they began talking . . . and dating! There were rumors of their relationship and a few photos, but the story really blew up when Taylor was seen at a Chiefs game on September 23. She sat in a box in Kansas City with Donna Kelce. TV cameras

caught Taylor cheering when Travis scored a touchdown as the Chiefs beat the Chicago Bears 41–13. The couple drove away after the game in Travis's car as photographers clicked away. "It was definitely a game I'll remember, that's for sure," said Travis. "Then we just slid off in the getaway car at the end."

A week later, Taylor was at the Chiefs game against the New York Jets in New Jersey. She sat with Donna Kelce again but was joined by fellow celebrities like Ryan Reynolds, Blake Lively, and Hugh Jackman. Was this a football game or the Oscars?

By then the secret was out, and social media exploded. Taylor went to several more games, always getting TV time and nearly always watching Travis and the Chiefs win. Coming off their Super Bowl championship, the team had their eyes on going back-to-back.

On October 15, the pair made surprise appearances on *SNL*. Afterward, photos showed them holding hands . . . and those photos quickly sped around the globe! In early November, the Chiefs had a week off. Taylor did not; as she was performing in far-off Buenos Aires, Argentina. In the audience after a long flight? Travis himself.

"I love it when Taylor comes and supports me and enjoys the game with the fam and friends," Travis said in one interview. "It's been nothing but a wonderful year, man."

WHERE DOES TRAVIS FIT?

Here's a list of our picks for the top tight ends of all time in the NFL. Do you think Travis should move up or down? It's just an opinion . . . not a fact! You can look up more stats about these players and make your own decision.

(Note: * means they are in the Pro Football Hall of Fame).

- Tony Gonzalez*: 1,325 catches, third all-time among all receivers
- Antonio Gates: 116 TD catches, most among tight ends
- Travis Kelce: Record seven straight 1,000-yard seasons, 3 Super Bowl wins
- Rob Gronkowski: 4 Super Bowl wins, 23 play-off TD catches
- Shannon Sharpe*: 3 Super Bowl wins, 8 Pro Bowl selections
- Kellen Winslow*: Set the standard for modern tight ends, 5 Pro Bowls

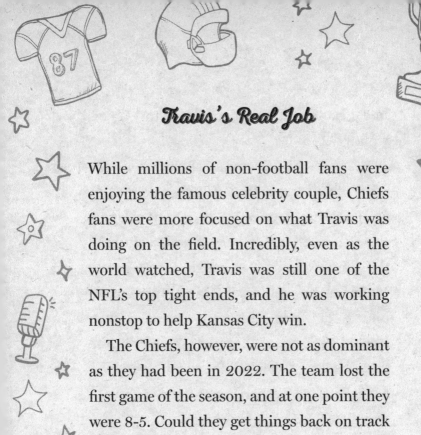

Travis's Real Job

While millions of non-football fans were enjoying the famous celebrity couple, Chiefs fans were more focused on what Travis was doing on the field. Incredibly, even as the world watched, Travis was still one of the NFL's top tight ends, and he was working nonstop to help Kansas City win.

The Chiefs, however, were not as dominant as they had been in 2022. The team lost the first game of the season, and at one point they were 8-5. Could they get things back on track and return to the Super Bowl?

After a shocking loss to the Las Vegas Raiders, the Chiefs rallied. They won their next five games in a row, including three playoff games. After beating Miami in the wild-card round, the Chiefs faced off against a key rival, the Buffalo Bills. Travis had two touchdown catches as the Chiefs won 27–24.

In the AFC Championship Game, the Chiefs faced the Baltimore Ravens and NFL MVP QB Lamar Jackson. It was a tough battle, but Travis made sure it ended up with the Chiefs on top. He caught all 11 passes Mahomes threw his way. One of them made him the all-time NFL leader in postseason catches (he had 165 through the end of the 2023 playoffs). The Chiefs won 17–10 and headed to their second Super Bowl in a row— and their fourth in five seasons.

As the Super Bowl approached, the Taylor and Travis Story got even bigger if you can believe that. While Travis was used to attention as an NFL superstar, the attention he got from being with Taylor was stratospheric. One newspaper even reported that men were flocking to barbershops, asking to get Travis's haircut!

Travis, however, knew how to stay on track, even as he enjoyed his new relationship with Taylor. "As long as we're happy, we can't listen to anything that's outside noise," he said. "That's all that matters. I brought this upon myself, and I do enjoy having fun with it all, and the biggest thing is making sure my focus is right here in this building."

His teammates knew that Travis would be able to tune out the "noise." Said Mahomes, "Travis is definitely my closest teammate. I would say our friendship is more like a brotherhood—we're brothers now and our families get along together. I'm part of his family and he's part of mine."

Still, said Travis, "It's been a wild year, man. Being famous worldwide is a lot different than being famous in Kansas City."

Travis's family knew that he could handle the pressure. "My boys know where they're from," said Ed Kelce. "They understand that how you treat people is what's important in this world. As long as that's how they think, I'm a happy guy."

It sounds like Travis still does think like that. He was asked at the Super Bowl in Las Vegas why everyone is so excited about him and Taylor being together. "I think it's the values we stand for," he said. "Who we are as people. We love to shine a light on others, shine a light on the people that love and support us. I feel like we both have a love for life."

BIGGEST SUPER BOWL MOMENTS

- ⬭ First Super Bowl TD: vs. 49ers, 2020

- ⬭ Sets Super Bowl Receiving Yards TE Record: vs. Buccaneers, 2021

- ⬭ Big Play to Set up Winning FG: vs. Eagles, 2022

- ⬭ Big Play in OT to Set Up Winning TD: vs. 49ers 2023

A Super Super Bowl

The night before the game, Travis spoke to the Chiefs. As one of their veteran leaders, he wanted to fire up his teammates. He told them they had to ignore all the outside "noise," just as he was trying to do. He pointed out that the Chiefs were the underdogs. That is, football experts were picking the 49ers to win. Travis would have none of that and he made his point . . . loudly!

The first three quarters of Super Bowl LVIII, once again against the 49ers, were actually pretty boring. Both teams made mistakes and missed chances. The 49ers looked a bit better and led 10–3 at halftime. The Chiefs got some points back early in the third quarter with another field goal. Then the team got a huge break. A Chiefs punt hit a 49ers player and Kansas City recovered the ball.

On the next play, the Chiefs took their first lead of the game on a Mahomes TD pass to Marquez Valdes-Scantling. But the 49ers moved quickly back into the lead on a TD pass by Brock Purdy.

In the fourth quarter, neither team could reach the end zone, but the kickers did great work. The 49ers' Jake Moody made a 53-yard field goal to put SF on top with less than two minutes to go. Kansas City needed to get at least a field goal or San Francisco would win. Fans were thrilled by the back-and-forth action (and yes, Taylor was in the stands to watch and cheer!). Mahomes once again led the way, and Travis made his biggest play of the game. With just 16 seconds left, he caught a pass and rumbled 22 yards to the 49ers' 11-yard line. That made Butker's job easy, and he tied the score again at 19–19.

For only the second time ever, the Super Bowl headed into overtime! A boring game had turned into a thriller!

San Francisco got the ball first. They drove down and scored a field goal. Mahomes and Travis and the Chiefs had to at least match that or else the 49ers would win. If the Chiefs could score a TD, however, KC would win.

Play by play, run by run, pass by pass, the Chiefs marched down the field. It looked like they might have to settle for a field goal and another tie. But Travis had one more big play in him. He took a pass from Mahomes and smashed his way to the 49ers' three-yard line. It took four defenders to bring him down! But it put the Chiefs in a perfect spot.

Calling a play named "Tom and Jerry," Mahomes rolled to his right. As two 49ers raced to cover Travis, the team's biggest threat, wide receiver Mecole Hardman was wide open. Mahomes hit him with a TD pass

FUN FACT

Superstition! Travis wears a small band of rubber on his left wrist for every game. He's worn it since 2020 and says he feels "naked" without it.

and that was it. Chiefs 25, 49ers 22! Another championship for Travis! He threw his arms in the air to celebrate and began hugging everyone in a red jersey.

Soon after he said, "To find a way through adversity yet again for four—actually, five—quarters, man, I couldn't be more proud of these guys. Being on the mountaintop with my brothers again, it brings tears to my eyes . . . I'm on top of the world."

And yes, Travis and Taylor met on the field and kissed as the world watched. It was a dream ending to the most amazing season of Travis's fantastic NFL career. Not long after Travis's Super Bowl win, Jason announced the end of his own time in the NFL. In a farewell speech, he said, "There is no chance I'd be here without the bond Travis and I share. It made me stronger, tougher, smarter, and it taught me the values of cooperation, loyalty, patience, and understanding."

Even if he had never met Taylor Swift, Travis Kelce would be among the most famous and successful NFL players of all time. He now has the most catches and second most receiving yards and touchdown catches in NFL postseason history. He owns three Super Bowl rings and is certain to join the Pro Football Hall of Fame in the future.

For now, though, his focus is back where he knows it belongs—on the field helping the Chiefs win. Of course, he also knows he has the loving support of a certain very talented singer. Stay tuned for the next chapters of the Travis and Taylor Show!

TIMELINE

2024

Travis Kelce wins third
Super Bowl (after 2023
season) over the 49ers

2023

Hosts *Saturday Night Live*
in March; starts dating
Taylor Swift in summer

2023

Wins second Super Bowl
(after 2022 season)
over the Eagles and
brother Jason

2020

Sets all-time record for
tight ends with 1,416
receiving yards in
2020 season

2020

Wins first Super Bowl
(after 2019 season) over
the 49ers

2016

Makes dating reality show,
Catching Kelce

2015

Makes the first of his nine
Pro Bowl teams.

2013

Chosen by the Kansas City
Chiefs in the third round
of the NFL Draft

2012

After missing 2010 season
on suspension, returns
to set Cincinnati receiving
records

2008

Begins college career as
redshirt freshman at
University of Cincinnati.

1989

Born on October 5 in
Westlake, Ohio